A COLOUR FOR SOLITUDE

SUJATA BHATT was born in Ahmedabad, India, in 1956. She is a graduate of the Writers' Workshop, University of Iowa and now lives in Germany with her husband and daughter. She has worked in the United States and in Canada, where she was the Lansdowne Visiting Writer at the University of Victoria, British Columbia. Carcanet publish her first four collections, *Brunizem* (Alice Hunt Bartlett Prize, Commonwealth Poetry Prize, 1988), *Monkey Shadows* (Poetry Book Society Recommendation, 1991), *The Stinking Rose* (1995), *Augatora* (Poetry Book Society Recommendation, 2000) and a substantial selected poems, *Point No Point* (1997). Her poems have been widely anthologized and have been translated into more than a dozen languages. She received a Cholmondeley Award in 1991 and the Italian Tratti Poetry Prize in 2000.

'Sujata Bhatt's brightly coloured, richly scented world is never more intelligent or ambitious in its reach than here in this new collection, *Augatora*.'

Maura Dooley, Poetry Book Society Bulletin

Also by Sujata Bhatt from Carcanet

Brunizem
Monkey Shadows
The Stinking Rose
Point No Point
Augatora

SUJATA BHATT

A Colour for Solitude

CARCANET

First published in 2002 by
Carcanet Press Limited
4th Floor, Conavon Court
12-16 Blackfriars Street
Manchester M3 5BQ

A CIP catalogue record for this book
is available from the British Library

ISBN 1 85754 589 3 (trade paperback)
ISBN 1 85754 594 X (hardback edition)
ISBN 1 85754 593 1 (limited edition)

The publisher acknowledges financial assistance
from the Arts Council of England

Set in 10pt Palatino by Bryan Williamson, Frome
Printed and bound in England by SRP Ltd, Exeter

for Michael and Jenny Mira

Acknowledgements

Thanks are due to the editors of the following publications in which some of these poems, sometimes in different versions, first appeared: *Poetry London, PN Review,* (UK); *Journal of Literature & Aesthetics* (India); *DiVersi Racconti, Vietri International Poetry Festival Anthology* (Italy).

'No Road Leads to This' and 'Was it the Blue Irises?' first appeared under different titles in *Brunizem*. 'Self-Portrait on My Fifth Wedding Anniversary, 25-5-06' first appeared under a different title in *The Stinking Rose*.

I am very grateful to Mahzarin Banaji, Chris Gribble, Jenny Leach and Eleanor Wilner for their helpful comments.

Special thanks to Andrea Sirotti and Paola Splendore for translating some of these poems into Italian.

Many thanks to Hille Darjes and to the late Tille Modersohn for their generous hospitality and friendship.

Thanks to the Paula Modersohn-Becker Museum for their assistance and encouragement over the years.

Contents

7

Author's Note

On a cold morning in March 1985, I visited the *Kunsthalle Bremen* for the first time – indeed it was my very first visit to Germany. And it was there in the *Kunsthalle* that I had my initial encounter with Paula Modersohn-Becker's paintings. I knew of Modersohn-Becker (1876–1907) through Rilke's famous poem 'Requiem for a Friend' which he had written for her in 1908. And I knew that she had also been a close friend of Rilke's wife, the sculptor Clara Rilke-Westhoff (1878–1954). Aside from that, however, I did not know much about Modersohn-Becker's life, nor did I know about the importance of her contribution to German and European art.

The first true modernist in German art, her work defies all attempts at categorisation. However 'simple' and straightforward Modersohn-Becker's subject or approach, the result is always unusual and frequently provocative. She discovered Cézanne's work for herself in Paris in 1900 before he was famous. Her work was open to influences from many artists such as Maillol, Gauguin, Rousseau, van Gogh, as well as the ancient Faiyum painters of Egypt. This is not to imply that her work was derivative. Instead, she transformed these influences within her work and made them her own. Some of her last paintings are said to anticipate Picasso's work: works by Picasso she would not have seen because she was already dead by then. Equally modern and sensitive in her life, Paula Modersohn-Becker's beliefs had nothing to do with dogmas or ideologies. Today, she is considered by many to be the most significant German woman painter of the twentieth century.

Modersohn-Becker died in 1907 at the age of thirty-one, of embolism, eighteen days after giving birth to her only child, a daughter. She left behind a vast body of work. During the last seven years of her life (which exclude her early years of study) she produced 560 paintings, 700 drawings and 13 etchings. Early critical response to her work was hostile. Fortunately, there were those such as Gustav Pauli (director of the *Kunsthalle Bremen*) and the German sculptor Bernhard Hoetger who recognised her genius and supported her work. Soon after Hitler came to power, Modersohn-Becker's paintings were *entartet*, condemned by the Nazis for being 'degenerate'. The Nazis confiscated some of her paintings (those that were in German museums) and sold them abroad, mainly to museums in the United States. The bulk of her work was hidden 'illegally' by friends and by her daughter – thus saving them (the paintings) from harm during the Third Reich. During her lifetime, Modersohn-Becker sold only three or at most four paintings. Rilke, impressed by her work, was the first to buy one of her paintings in 1905: *Säugling mit der Hand der Mutter, 1903*, (Infant with its Mother's Hand) in an act of genuine friendship and out of his wish to encourage her and to provide practical support for her work during a time when she had decided to leave her husband, Otto Modersohn.

It has been only in the last twenty-five years or so that Paula Modersohn-Becker's work has gained, however slowly, the respect it has been deprived of. And yet, she is still largely unknown to the general public outside Germany.

To return to that March day in 1985: from the beginning, I was very moved and struck by Modersohn-Becker's paintings. Two weeks later, I returned to Iowa where I was a student at the time and almost immediately wrote my first poem in response to one of her self-portraits. It is now entitled 'Was it the Blue Irises?' and was first published in *Brunizem*.

Much later, after I received my degree, I married my German friend, the writer Michael Augustin who had invited me to Bremen in the first place. And then, I started to live in Germany.

My interest in Modersohn-Becker can be traced to Clara Rilke-Westhoff (whose friend she was) and ultimately to Rilke and to Rilke's work. I had started reading Rilke's poems in 1974. Then, very much under his spell and keen on reading everything he had written, I turned to his letters and journals. Soon, I became aware of Clara's presence and especially of her silence. Her silence, the fact that she had not left any extensive written record of her feelings, (to my knowledge then), considering her problematic relationship with Rilke and given Rilke's verbal expansiveness, intrigued me and it bothered me. Clara's silence inspired me to break that silence and to imagine what she might have said. I wrote my first poem in Clara's voice in 1979. This poem, now entitled 'No Road Leads to This' (first published in *Brunizem*) grew out of my desire to give life to Rilke's abstract notion of love as 'two solitudes greeting and saluting each other'. At that time, (1979), of course, I had never been to Germany and so did not have a clue as to what Worpswede looked like. Maps, pictures and written descriptions of the place proved to be useful. Ultimately, however, the physical world I created in the poem had to be imagined. Little did I know that many years later, I would be living just a few miles away from Worpswede, in the immediate neighbourhood of the *Kunsthalle Bremen* which accomodates the works of the major Worpswede artists, including Clara Rilke-Westhoff.

Clara Rilke-Westhoff was a sculptor at a time when it was unheard of for women to engage in such strenuous artistic work. Indeed, in those days, the word *'Bildhauerin'* (sculptress) sounded ridiculous to German ears. However, she quickly won the respect and admiration of her teachers, Max Klinger and Auguste Rodin. In fact, it was through Clara that Rilke became acquainted with Rodin. Clara Rilke-Westhoff's work is even more unknown than that of Modersohn-Becker's. Owing to her continual financial difficulties, she could not always afford the materials for her work and so she produced relatively few pieces of sculpture. She is most famous for her remarkable busts of Rilke, especially the one created in 1905, which Rodin admired tremendously.

In 1994, after I wrote my second poem connected with another Modersohn-Becker self-portrait, now entitled 'Self-Portrait on My Fifth Wedding Anniversary, 25-5-06' (first published in *The Stinking Rose*), I thought of eventually writing a sequence of poems entirely devoted to and drawing their inspiration from Paula Modersohn-Becker's paintings, especially the self-portraits of which there are more than fifty and which appear at every stage of Modersohn-Becker's artistic development. By that time (1994), I was long familiar with Paula's biography and with her letters and journals. The German language itself had a new resonance for me as I watched my small daughter grow up. (More recently, listening to her learn and recite Rilke's poems for school has added another dimension to my relationship with Rilke's work.) My poems grew out of this atmosphere.

One does not usually associate poetry with research. I, however, find myself increasingly drawn to subjects that demand research: subjects that are either historical events or historical figures. Ironically, I find that the facts often free the imagination to probe deeper, to imagine things that otherwise could not have been imagined. Practically all of my research was conducted in German. However, since English is my language, the poems are in English. Paula and Clara, of course, had spoken in German to each other. And so, in a sense, there was always a certain amount of linguistic tension that I experienced in the making of this book. At the same time, there were days when I was not aware of the language I was working in. There were days when I was only aware of the sounds, rhythms, colours and emotions involved with my 'characters' or 'speakers'.

Over the years, I have been to many art exhibitions dealing with Modersohn-Becker and some of her more famous contemporaries in different parts of Germany and in other countries in Europe. Since my early days in Bremen, I have known the actress, Hille Darjes, who is Modersohn-Becker's grandniece. Hille's mother grew up with Paula's daughter, for it was Hille's grandmother, Milly Rohland-Becker, (Paula's sister), who looked after the newborn Mathilde right after Paula's death. Knowing Hille Darjes, who introduced me to Mathilde (Tille) Modersohn, has of course given me a more personal link with Paula Modersohn-Becker.

The book started with poems in response to Paula's paintings but then included Clara's sculptures and started to explore the close friendship between the two women. And then, the poems inevitably included Rilke and Paula's and Clara's perception of him, especially in connection with their portrayals of him in paint or in bronze. I say 'their' perception of Rilke, however, it is of course 'their perception' as I have imagined it. For although Paula's letters and journals have largely survived, there is a great deal she did not comment on. And when she was most deeply immersed in her painting, she left no written record of her thoughts. Here, I should add that Clara has not been entirely silent. Her private journals, however, still remain sealed and unavailable. Various people, including Paula, have recorded their memories of Clara and their conversations with her and I have found these memoirs useful in imagining Clara's voice. As a poet, I have been more interested in exploring and imagining what has been left unsaid and what has been left aside for speculation by biographers and art historians. Therefore, Clara's (and Paula's) relative silence has been more of an inspiration to me than a hindrance. Modersohn-Becker's own relationship with Rilke was also quite complex. Many biographers believe that Rilke married Clara Westhoff impulsively on the rebound when he learned that Paula was secretly engaged to the much older painter, Otto Modersohn. Paula herself was astonished by Rilke's decision to marry Clara and grew increasingly disillusioned as her own marriage disappointed her and as she felt Rilke prevented her from seeing Clara Westhoff, (her dearest friend), the way she had been accustomed to in the past. So far, to a large extent, Rilke has had the last word regarding both Clara and Paula. I wanted to change that, to restore the balance, so to speak.

My own life in Bremen and my frequent visits to Worpswede have no doubt entered the poems, even where it is not apparent. And my experience of the weather, the landscape, the language and the music of Northern Germany has surely affected my perception of the colours in Modersohn-Becker's paintings. At the same time, being the ultimate foreigner, I retain the perspective of an outsider. And perhaps to some extent, responding to Moder-sohn-Becker's work has been a way for my mind to enter and try to understand a totally alien culture and country. In the end, of course, there are the poems, just the poems, for there is a great deal that cannot be explained or analysed in rational, numerical terms, or even in prose.

SUJATA BHATT, 2001

Notes about the Text

1.   The titles of the poems responding to Modersohn-Becker's self-portraits and other paintings are in some cases taken from the paintings, however, in other cases, I have given them my own titles.

2.   Most of Modersohn-Becker's and Rilke-Westhoff's work can be found in museums in Bremen, Worpswede, Fischerhude and in other parts of Northern Germany.

3.   In the poems, partly for the sake of clarity, to avoid confusion, and partly out of a desire to restore their own, original identities to them (which incidentally, each in her own way tried to return to), I have referred to Paula Modersohn-Becker and Clara Rilke-Westhoff by their maiden names.

Im vergangenen Jahr schrieb ich: die Stärke, mit der ein Gegenstand aufgefaßt wird, das ist die Schönheit in der Kunst. Ist es nicht auch so in der Liebe?

Paula Modersohn-Becker

Last year I wrote: the intensity with which a subject is grasped, that is the beauty in art. Isn't this also true for love?

[author's translation]

Self-Portrait as Aubade
1897

The gaze in the mirror:
straightforward yet unconscious –
the self-assessment is open to the bone,
open to the soul –

Will the quest begin now?

Outside it is Berlin,
    it is 1897 –
the colours of a cold spring morning –

Will the quest begin now?

You are all-knowing but innocent.
Not smiling, not coy, not sad –
And your face: moonstone white –
blue-grey shadows make you
       almost marble, almost –
if it weren't for the wash of tan, the tinge
of beige beneath the white:
       colours of blanched almonds –

You are serious, wide-awake – already
no trace of sleep in your eyes –
A self-portrait as waiting for
         the aubade,
as waiting for you don't know what.

How long do you need to wait? How long
will you need – before the quest
        can truly begin?

Meanwhile, you give me
    yourself
waiting in front of the mirror:
      meanwhile
your green broken with black branches
enters the mirror – your green invites

17

the aubade – gives fragrance to your waiting –
however dark this green – your black
making it olive – however dark this green,
still, there is the fragrance
of a cold spring morning.

The gaze in the mirror is steady
and the part in your hair is so straight –

the green surrounds your moonstone skin –
            your memories of blanched almonds –

untouched and aching
            to be touched –

But you *are* the aubade
            and do not know it –

Self-Portrait done with Red Chalk
1897

You are Italian now –
    Renaissance sadness
in your eyes – seriousness
of the very young –

And red chalk your only colour
except for a few black shadows –
spidery in your hair –
        a few black strokes – strong enough
to cut the neckline of your dress –

You have made yourself
Italian – your face: smaller, narrower –
Red chalk colouring your concentration,
your deep attention – A pigment
        Faiyum painters used
only for the skin of men,
for the darker skin
            of men who worked outdoors –

But you do not know that –
            not yet.

Self-Portrait as My Sister
1897

Whose face is this?

An accident?

It is my sister, Herma
on a windy day –

The wind tears all shapes
into a blur of colour –

Even the lines of this face
            are scattered
as if the wind has flung
      Herma's face onto mine –
as if our faces were flowers
            in the wind's path –

Greens, yellows, reds
swirling into each other –
Only my Herma eyes remain steady:
coal black, fixed points
            unconcerned
in a landscape strewn
      with broken branches –

Self-Portrait with Coppery Red Hair
1897/98

The fire is in your hair –
still, you have found her:
            the older woman
who hides in your young face –
your twenty-two-year-old face.

Your skin is discoloured –
                your skin
is a thin eggshell – light seeps in –
pale light falls over the cracks –
        fragile, yellow –
your skin is parchment
                your skin is rice paper –
light seeps in –   ice clings to the window panes –
shadows of veins –   so blue –   shadows
  of bones almost jutting through –
and the mauve hairline cracks,
                filaments of burst capillaries –

Something made you
turn around and look up
with a sharp glance –   a bird of prey –
You are so gaunt
        and the old woman
living in your young face
                grows stronger –
  a bird of prey –   you are
not at all apologetic
for your hunger, your need –

Self-Portrait in Front of Window
Offering a View of Parisian Houses
1900

My face is distorted:
    so broad at the cheekbones,
a butterfly shape
    filled with the darkness
of indoors –
as if I were looking into
one of those mirrors
        those circus mirrors –

But I'll still look up as high as I can,
into the mirror – ignoring the windows
of the houses behind me –

Symmetry, symmetry – I can't forget –
Look at the large grey bow
tying up this blouse
       at my neck –

It is 1900. I had to begin
my new century in Paris.
I look like the perfect student
about to go for a walk.
I look too conventional.
It is 1900. I am numb –
    It is so dark –
the light is behind thick white clouds
behind the houses behind me –

And I stand waiting
for something to happen.

Shall I undo this bow,
      shall I
step out of my clothes?

Two Girls, Two Sisters
Paula Becker to Clara Westhoff, 1900

Two girls, two sisters –
    that's what Rilke calls us,
celebrating us – and he would join
    our sisterhood – If only we could
remain like this, Clara –
    open in our love
without having to choose –

A White Horse Grazing in Moonlight
1901

A mirage.

A horse from a fairy-tale.

So much light from the moon
so much silvery whiteness –
    and the earth
unearthly but fragrant
with lilies of the valley –

But the mirage is real.
The fairy-tale is true.

The white horse walks up to me
            fearless
and eats fresh grass
    out of my hands –

So love is fearless –
    it must be.

Your Weyerberg Gaze
Clara Westhoff's bust of Rilke, 1901
Clara Westhoff to Rainer Maria Rilke

I am heavy with child –
        I am slower –
and you are restless –

Clouds move across the sky –
leisurely at first, swelling out,
billowing like luxurious balloons
        getting larger and larger –
And then they break apart
                scattering –
and then they start racing
as if they were fleeing, anxious
        to get away
    from something terrible –
anxious to follow the birds
            into the future –

Cloud shadows fall
        across your face –

For once you are not reading,
not writing – and I can
enjoy your 'Weyerberg gaze'
as you stare down at the fields
from the hill – and then look up
            at the horizon –

This afternoon
as we sat drinking Chinese tea,
the scent of smoky jasmine
        filled our rooms –
a delicate, faint perfume –

And when you spoke
our child jumped within me
as if jolted out of a dream –
I could feel the arms and legs
so clearly – the growing fingers
the toes – so abrupt, that jabbing –
　　　You told me
to take a deep breath –
Breathe in the roses, you said –
breathe in the scent
　　　　　of these roses –
and now breathe in
the scent of your jasmine tea –

No Road Leads to This

Clara Westhoff to Rainer Maria Rilke, 1901
Westerwede

No road leads
to this old house we chose.
Its roof of straw scattered
by the loud wind wheezing
its North Sea sounds.
No road leads
to this old house we chose.

I live downstairs
with my clay and stones.
You upstairs
with ink and paper.
What do we do but play with truth,
a doll whose face
I must rework again and again
until it is human.
The clay has gathered all the warmth
from my hands. I am too cold
to touch the marble yet.

Last night the wind blew
my candle out. Tonight again
on the staircase, I
grope my way to your room.
Each night I climb
up these steps
back to you, with your open windows
so close to the wind and stars.
I listen to your poems as I wash
the dust off my skin and hair.
You must have the windows open all night,
I must watch
the straw from the roof
slowly swirl, fall inside
and gently cover your poems.

Tomorrow
come downstairs, will you,
it has been a month.
I want to show you
the new stone I found
stuck in the mud by the dead tree.
Such a smooth globe, not quite white
but honeydew
with a single dark green vein curled across.
Come downstairs, will you, see
the bright red leaves I stole from the woods;
see my lopsided clay
figure bow low down
before my untouched marble.
Tomorrow
come see the ground,
the gawky yellow weeds
at eye level from my window down below.

The Washing on the Line
1901

The wind is a ghost today
        possessing clothes –
practically wearing my camisole –
while the mauve tablecloth ripples
as if it were a field of flowers.

Wet clothes slap
      a cold spring wind –
slap a storm, pushing it
        into a stronger rage –

And now the wind turns
on me, howling deeper into
my ears, into the tender
        parts that hurt –
and deeper inside my head
there's a shrill whining, as if
the dead were calling out
        to me –

Two Girls in a Landscape
1901

The older one has straw blonde hair
with a tinge of flaxen green.
She is ten.
She has a cat's face,
almost – a cat's eyes – bluish grey
Siamese grey, slate grey, steel grey –
and the black pupils burn
              with scorn.
Her left eye is sharply crooked
as if hanging from a broken bone
                  an injured brow –
Her left eye is wounded
and all the bitterness
of her tears have made it
lopsided. Her younger sister
is four. She has strawberry blonde hair:
a pinkish halo. Her eyes are very round
and larger than her sister's.
Her eyes are dark brown
and so afraid.

The younger one clutches her sister,
holding on with a tight grip
as if to prevent her
              from fighting back.

It is Worpswede in 1901.
A summer evening – endless light –
The moon rising early –
long before the sunset is over –
a sunset that makes
the girls' faces rosy.

The landscape is green –
　　　It is the green of a fairy tale
for there is so much white
　　　mixed in with the green,
so much white that makes the green unreal.

But the girls are real.
The ten-year-old was just beaten,
her arm twisted for no good reason,
for money, for what she could surrender –

It was a man no doubt –
　　　father, uncle, brother – ?
The four-year-old ran away and hid.
The mother stayed behind
with the littlest one
　　　who cannot walk yet.

The landscape is placid
with a whitish green flatness.
The landscape is deaf
and blind – Still, the girl
with the cat's face
is not afraid as you paint
her wounds, her anger.
She stands motionless –
　　　upright, poised
just the way you want her –

But remember,
both of the girls are *you*, Paula –
and the landscape is Otto.

Icicles Hang from the Reeds of Our Roof
Clara Westhoff to Paula Becker, February 1902

Icicles hang
         from the reeds
of our roof –
My daughter is two months old now –

You are angry
at me, bitter – You say
I sound too much like Rainer.

But what is love?

Should love not be open –
         open to change,
open to the other?

Or do you love me more
because you don't
want me to change?

Self-Portrait with Scratches
1903

The scratches are intentional,
deliberate. This is your new method:
layer upon layer of paint –
             a muddy river –
and then you enter
with a sharp knife
to carve out the light.
To find light beneath silt, brine –
to find your first pale colours
swallowed by muddy paint.

Here is your clawed out light – pulled out
from somewhere deep inside the canvas.

Strokes that are short and fast,
so abrupt – leaving the surface
unsettled and yet intact.

Like the left wing of a blue jay
found in the grass – curled up as if
it were a fan of feathers, a swirling bouquet –
The feathers too fresh, too blue
to have fallen off – The feathers
too many to have been discarded
by one bird – But then the curve
    of the wing fits
in a woman's hand:
the bones unbroken
        the feathers unmarred –
not loose, not separate
but held together as a wing – intact –
Still, there is
clawed out light – The blue
scratched out of the jay – The wing
snapped off so cleanly – Was it a hawk
or a cat? Blueness of intense loss,
violence seeped into the feathers –

colours of startled eyes –
The scars are there
even if you cannot see them –
those marks made into the earth.

This is the face of a fourteen-year-old girl.
Why have you taken it as yours?
For you are twenty-seven –
Why? Why is it so dark?
Even your necklace is muddy,
    struggling to be seen
above the high collar
    of your white shirt.
Why is this you
looking like a fourteen-year-old girl
after two years of marriage?
Why the scratches, the clawed out light?

What is the movement
        behind these marks?

If only he had known
    how to touch you –
If only Otto had –
If only Rilke had –
If only you could have whispered:
'Rainer!'
If only you could have shown him –
If only you could have shown
Otto –

There was a man
        who could catch fish
with his bare hands
        if he wanted to.
He could catch birds, songbirds –
Songbirds crushed in his fists
            if he wanted to –
That was a story in Paris.
He was a sailor from Goa.
That was the movement

behind the scratches, the clawed out light –
That was *your* movement – the way you entered
the canvas with a knife –
        scarring yourself
into a fourteen-year-old face –

Self-Portrait with Blossoming Trees
1903

And if I paint myself serene
      will I become
serene – at one with these
        blossoming trees?

And if I sign my name
      as 'Paula Modersohn'
in large capital letters,
       will I feel more
like Otto's wife?

It is the light that melts
into me – the trees behind me
throw their fragrance over
my hair – and the way I stand
it looks as if the flowers are growing
out of my head – yellowish white petals
sparkling and moist – how they form
a thick white halo – my face takes on
their joy, *their* bliss –

I can smile only because
it is spring – because the blueness
    of this sky
opens my soul –

Two Girls: The Blind Sister
1903

My blind sister
    stands in the sun.

I stand behind her.
    I hold her, guide her –

Look at her pale yellow eyelashes,
the blonde hairs of her eyebrows –

Today, the sun will not
        let her hide –

Birdsong echoes within her mind –

Birdcalls trapped
    beneath her eyelids –

Her eyelids: so translucent –

Her eyelids flicker, they tremble –

Her eyelids throb
    as if they contained
the hearts of birds –

Self-Portrait in Front of a Landscape with Trees
1903

I walk over bones
          in the mud
over clumps of grass
torn by those who came here
before – hoof prints filled with rainwater –
Even my wooden shoes
          sink in, get stuck.

In a dark brown dress
          of sturdy cotton,
I can become
a part of the landscape –

Here is a face
the earth is trying to take back.

A strand of my hair
joins the trunk of a tree.

The sky is white – endless bone
as if it were a vast skull –
          Air so thick
I can hardly breathe.
     Dusty, damp spores
shed by birch trees – their leaves
          stunned into silence.

All the light there is
is taken by my bone-white brooch.

Linden trees dazed
into a greenish blue trance.
A heavy darkness –
          they too struggle
against the air –

Browns and maroons
    at the end of August –
faraway, a dun horse –
    faraway and everywhere
the colour of chestnuts
on a dark day – the colour
    of dried blood –

These colours need blue
        and orange –
But they must have blue.
How they try to live,
to be something more –

Two Girls in Profile in a Landscape
charcoal, 1903/04

Now the dark sister is thinner, taller –
She cries out in horror
for she has witnessed
something – she does not know
how to describe it – too simple
to call it death, for it is more
than death – Evil, pure evil,
and yet, only from her perspective
is it evil – The brutality of what
    she has seen
distorts her eyes, brings fear
into her face – She tries
to explain but does not know
      how to begin –
Her younger sister smiles, lost
in another dream – Her blondeness
shines in the sun – She smiles
unaware that her older sister
is stuttering again, unaware
that something needs to be said –
Look, she is almost skipping, she is
in such a hurry to get away,
    far away
into an open meadow
      rustling with new grass –
The older sister follows, stumbling along –
unable to find the right words –
But the younger sister is already
thinking of the wildflowers
    she wants to gather –
  already thinking
of a white horse she wants to greet –

In Her Green Dress, She is
1905

In her green dress, she is
the background and the foreground –

A green dress the colour
        of iris stems,
the ones in the background –

A green dress
    the colour of iris stems against grass –

Green on green on green –

She is the foreground
    and the background –

Her face intent because
she's listening to a bird in the distance –
        a single bird – persistent –
calling again and again –
Its song slit, cleft –
            rising and falling
and rising again through the stillness.
Its song clinging to the leaves –
        A melody
that must have moved Bach –

Her face intent because irises
have flung themselves open in the heat:
Blue petals arched
like so many little blue tongues
                tasting the air –

Those yellow hearts cannot hide anymore.

Even the black stones, the oval shaped
black stones of her necklace
            can see you –

It is June: Full of humid shadows,
purple clouds – it will rain
in an hour. The irises will sway
in the wind – a few stems will
get bent by the rain – broken –
and her green dress will get drenched
        along with the grass
where the stems will lie
                    broken –

But she will walk away
laughing – she will walk slowly
lingering in the green wetness –

Self-Portrait with Your Jaw Set
1905

If truth is impossible
then are you good
at telling lies?

Woman of Pompeii, of ancient Pompeii,
you have made yourself
so regal, almost matronly
            with three children at home.

But yours is the face in the mosaic –
Yours is the face in the fresco.

Liquid gold
  thick around your throat –

And the gold is everywhere:
            flickering in your eyes
washed across your hair –

Your jaw set
  against Vesuvius –

Pompeii glancing out of your eyes
as if you were about to say,
            'I dare you –'

You are the Rose
Clara Westhoff's bust of Rilke, 1905
Clara Westhoff to Rainer Maria Rilke

On the terrace
　　of Schloß Friedelhausen
you sat with your head bowed
　　reading as if you were praying –
Your soft neck
　　　so exposed –
Vulnerable, frail – a bent flower stem
　　　about to break –

And then I knew:
　　it is *you* –
You are the rose.
And all your life
　　you will seek
the perfect gardener.

You sat with your head bowed,
bent forward, stooping, awkward –
　　your face spilling into your book –

Was your mind filled with prayers –
with blessings waiting to be uttered?

Countess Luise von Schwerin was too ill
　　to sit for me – What could I do
but model you – There on the terrace
you were so far away from me –
You did not know me anymore
and so I could see you
　　　　for what you are –

Afterwards
I arranged and rearranged
　　the position of your head,
the vulnerability of your neck –

And in the end
I placed you on my podium
    with *your* gesture:
  the way you place
and replace a single rose
in your slender, silver vase –

A Red Rose in November
Paula Becker to Clara Westhoff, 1905

Forget Rilke –
   the way he left you –

I must remind you
of your strength –
These November mornings
as I paint you
in your white dress –
I must remind you
    of your power –

Your small daughter,
almost four, runs between us,
    laughing –
how she plays on the floor
while I study your white dress
      soaking up
the last light of the year.

Still, some mornings at eleven
the sun blazes as if
      it were June –

And now when I look
at your face – I know,
again, you are dreaming
    of Rodin,
the garden at Meudon – what luck –
The weeks you spent
working by his side – your hands
raw from the wet clay,
your fingers cracked
and bruised from chiselling stone –
    But of course, you smile –

At first, I wanted you
in profile – you have a face
that should be carved in stone.

But now when you sit like this,
with your head tilted to the side,
and your eyes turned away
from me – your eyes turned
to the window, to the sky –
when you sit like this
            remembering Rodin –
I can look at you fully,
deeply – without you observing me –
I need you to look away from me.
I need to watch you,
    to grasp you
without your gaze
interrupting mine – without your gaze
            blocking mine –

The red rose is full
            and yet frail
in your large hand –
How your dark hair takes in the red –
while the rose breathes in the darkness
            from your hair –

When I painted the lines of your neck
I thought of the day we rung
the church bells endlessly –
How you pulled on the rope
            of the bigger bell
and I, beside you ringing the smaller one –
we swung along with the bells –
lifted way up, our feet off the floor,
we held on to the ropes –
our white dresses billowing up
and down, we swung along
            over and over–
we couldn't stop –
the whole village alarmed,
frightened and then angry at us –

That was years ago –
but I want to paint what we felt
on that day – the sounds
            of the bells –
I want to paint *that* into the shadows
                  across your neck.

You were always the strong one –
spontaneous – pregnant before
            your wedding day –

Nowadays
you look at me puzzled –
you cannot understand
why I have no child – 'Why not
if you want one?' your eyes
      always ask –

How can I tell you the truth?
How shall I say it?
That in the fifth year of my marriage
I am still untouched – a virgin –
still Paula Becker – Otto has not
      made me his wife.
I don't know if he cannot or will not –

And I don't know how
to speak of it – even to you –

Don't Look at Me like That
Clara Westhoff to Paula Becker, 1905

Don't look at me
like that – Sometimes your glance
    is too sharp.

This morning
as I sat in your atelier,
a part of me was afraid.
I clenched my teeth
as you scrutinized me,
as your eyes scoured
      over me –

But in the end you retrieved me
    from my abyss.

You made me greater
than I am – my skin
the skin of a stone goddess –

its texture rich
    with centuries
      of sun and rain –

Self-Portrait with an Oversized Hat and a Red Rose in the Right Hand
1905

In reality I am diminished.

My shoulders have shrunk:
narrow, narrow, they cannot
            get any smaller –

In reality there are moments
of resignation – Long moments
that keep spilling over
            into the future –

You have to look hard
        into the shadows cast
by this huge hat –
You have to strain your eyes
            to find mine.

Only my hands maintain
their strength – They pulse
and itch, anxious to continue –

A red rose bleeds
        into my white dress –
The petals are wounded –
and my own wound
        is a dark red rose –

In reality I pretend
        to be strong
when I am not –

And now this hat
        wants to suck me out
            of my grief –

Self-Portrait with a Necklace of White Beads
1906

This mouth is preparing itself
to speak French again.

See how my lips have changed
their shape: fuller, softer –
            even my words
are more resilient.

It's still January
but the days are truly mild.
I rise before the sky
            gets pink –
And today
I'm dressed for spring.

I wear a flimsy brown dress
            with scarlet dots –
And these white beads,
this necklace worn in haste
doesn't really fit.

This dress requires
a slender chain of gold
or a collar made of bright coral.

And yet, the white beads are perfect:
They make the scarlet
            sharper –

But who cares.
In a month I'll be gone.
I may never see Worpswede again.
And Otto – how can I bear
            to face him
after I leave this time –

Let the scarlet grow sharper
against the white beads –

This mouth is preparing itself
to speak French forever –

Self-Portrait with a Wreath of Red Flowers
in Your Hair
1906

You have just eaten strawberries –
    wild ones that were small
but sweet. You have found
a lover, you have found love –
    but no one believes you.

A wreath of red flowers, a crown
brings out the brown shadows in your hair.

You are a Viking Queen.
Your mouth is crimson, redder than anything.

And the whites of your eyes
are filled with the colour
of cut forget-me-nots –

Cut forget-me-nots in a jar
after two days in the May sun –

While more strawberries
are ripening and you have just
found a lover – you keep
    reminding yourself.

The blue fading, yet brightening to white –
    The blue changing –
Yet the blue still fresh
as if it were not truly dying
but being diluted by all
the water sucked up by the stems –

One thinks the forget-me-nots
will live forever – as the tiny flowers
get paler everyday –
    and the leaves stay green –

You say the juice
of forget-me-nots can be used
to strengthen iron.
But no one believes you.

The crown of red flowers, high
on your head, mingles
into your hair – making you
        restless – a Viking Queen
about to set off
        on a long journey.

And these are the flowers you didn't include
in the picture: Fat jam jars full
of forget-me-nots pulled out from the garden,
                torn away from the earth
to make space for other flowers.

Handfuls of thick bundles:
Two jam jars on the windowsill
one on the table – pine wood –
Your lover already far away
        but waiting for you.

Now these flowers you didn't paint,
the forget-me-nots
        spill out of your eyes –

A Colour for Solitude
Paula Becker to Rainer Maria Rilke, 1906

Of course I know
    your eyes are blue –
So blue that I almost married you –
So blue, so heroic,
        it still hurts
to stare you down.

But that is not the point.

The point is today
your eyes got so dark
when you saw me alone,
simply standing by the window
in my amber necklace.

Why should I not hint
at your weak chin – why should I not
reveal your mouth
        as I have seen it?

Truth does not belong
to you alone – Truth does not
belong to anyone.

Maybe this portrait
that I'm making of you
is more intimate than sex –

All these hours we spend together
in my room – while all of Paris
stays locked outside.
No one has dared
to see you the way I have.

All these hours I am the artist:
For once, it is me who is
not female, not male – but both
and also neither – I am the artist
who understands the light on your skin.

Nights I sleep with my paintings around me.
But most of all, I keep
your portrait in my mind, my dreams –

What can I offer you that is more
honest, more passionate?
Look, here is my secret,
        look, I have hidden it
beneath your tongue –
Your tongue that no one can see
in this portrait I have done –
your tongue, there, inside
the darkness of your eternally open mouth.

And when we kissed,
        just now,
did you think of the lilies
        in my old atelier? Did you
remember our early days in Worpswede?
How we denied
our love for each other –
The hours we spent talking –
the hot cups of tea – endless
and steaming in our hands –
The hours we spent
talking against the constant sound of rain –
the rain falling – gently, persistently –
The candles I lit
        to welcome your words –
How we loved each other
those last days before
each of us married the wrong beloved –

And when we kissed
        this morning,
watched by all the eyes
        in my paintings –
did you think we were still
two artists, two misunderstood
solitudes trying to protect each other?

Or were we simply a man and a woman
unable to let go of each other – ?
And yet always unable
to stand undressed before each other.

Is it love we should give each other?
Is it sex? I don't know.
And yet, I know a part of me
has always loved you –
has always been afraid
of loving you – I could never be
the rose in your poems –
        the sleeping girl –
I could never be so innocent
                and so motionless.
And you could never fit in
with the trees in my landscapes
the colours in my skies –

But don't you see,
now in this portrait
I'm trying to say:
Look, I have seen you naked,
more naked than anyone else has seen you –
And this time, I do not flinch
from the confusion in your eyes.

I must tell you,
this portrait shall remain
the way it is – It is finished
in its unfinishedness.
And I cannot
        paint your eyes blue
until you can show me

how to live for art – for the greatness
of art – without guilt.
Show me
how you live out desire, live out
every urgent desire –
and yet, always remain true
            to yourself.

Give me
a better colour
    for solitude –

Self-Portrait on My Fifth Wedding Anniversary
25-5-06

I will become amber.

Daphne wanted
to become a tree.
I think
it was she who chose sweet laurel,
she who chose leaves that are always green.

But I need to go
deeper, into amber.

Already this light,
this sunny May morning
          in Paris
has turned my hair amber
          the dark russet kind –
more red than gold.

My eyes: brownish amber
sparkle brighter than the necklace
I wear today – large oval
beads of amber – so heavy.

It's too warm, too early,
but never mind. I'm half-naked. It's easier
to paint what I mean to paint
          this naked way.

How would I look
if I were pregnant?
Like this? My nipples, still so pale
would also turn to amber.

And my blood?
I imagine it too will become stronger.
It will stop its rush-rush river sounds
it will stop pounding
my blood will become quiet
        silent –
and in the end
it will harden into amber.

My belly is so white!
So white!
How round should I make it?
How big will I get
when I'm with child?

Oh I will paint it round enough
so there will be no doubt
about my condition.

This is a self-portrait
of a pregnant woman
who secretly knows
she will become amber.

This is a self-portrait
in which I don't care
what anyone says.

Exactly five years ago today
we got married – Otto and I.
But this May I am alone
at last with my *self*.
My *self* that now only speaks
to me in Paris.

I need to live
        more fully through
the body to find my soul.

Yes, the body, this woman's body
                    that is mine –
I need to go deeper
into amber.

Should I have a baby?
And if I did?
Then, would my body be able
to teach my soul something new?

Self-Portrait as a Nude Torso
with an Amber Necklace
1906

This is my soul:
A nude with Buddha's smile.

Yes, even Buddha's smile
     can be mine.

I stand with a flower
     in each hand –
Flowers shaped like my nipples.

But the flowers are smaller
with dark green centres,
     night green stems.

The flowers are bluish pink –
my nipples are pinkish orange.

This is my soul: Pure roundness –
Beads of pure amber –
It is me and yet beyond me.

How I hold these flowers:
my left hand is a vase
full of shadow – my right hand
     is full of movement –
my arms, geometric, as in a dance –
almost encircling my solar plexus –
     My soul protecting itself.

My soul's eyes see you
     and they don't.

There are white and orange butterflies
everywhere – and more flowers
in my hair, flowers at my feet
     that you can't see.

I stand in front of tall ferns.

The sun is right on me.

What is there? What
is there behind those ferns? You ask –

Such dark ferns – all colours
are dark over here.

This is my soul:
It is more than me.

And behind these ferns that reach and reach
almost blocking out the sky –
behind these ferns
            full of butterflies

pinkish red flamingos step
into water – There is a lake.

And further away
leopards sleep
            hidden within trees –

Self-Portrait as Anonymous
1906

You are one of many, you are all three
              women over here –
You are Isis in the middle
              of a dance –

And you are not.

Clara is there
approaching you from the background –
her face so clear in profile.
The red tulip in her hand
              also clear cut,
chiselled as sharp as her face –

Let the third woman
              remain unknown –

The third woman who looks up
at the moon, who cries out
              so we know the drums
are getting louder –

We know who you are, we know
              where you are –
and yet, we do not.

You Spoke of Italy
Paula Becker to Rainer Maria Rilke, 1906

Rainer, dear friend, I cannot
sleep tonight – and I do not want to sleep.

I've been trying on
those dresses and evening gowns
and those undergarments
        made of silk
that you helped me choose
yesterday at the shop –
The packages arrived this morning.

Such blues and greens
glistening as if they were
        perpetually wet –
Such reds smouldering with love,
        with ripeness –
I will memorize myself
in these clothes, these riches of Koré –
        unearthly colours – jewels
I can never pay for.

Tomorrow
I will send everything back.

But for tonight
        it is all mine –
I might even sleep in silk –

I pace before the mirror
and I keep thinking
of our evening together –

Your simple, meatless dinner
that you shared with me –
And afterwards, the strawberries –
I felt so pure, so free – you watching
me while I watched you –
Your small hands

I always found so moving –
You were sweet and pale, your skin
        smelling of almonds –
How you spoke of Italy –
of Florence, Capri – How you spoke
        of a journey
we should make together –
I only interrupted to say, with Clara,
with Clara, let us be three again –
And as I listened
        to your stories
I remembered the scent of fresh lemons
and especially the leaves
                    with their different fragrance
        with their rough dark green
softened by that fragrance –

Is there More Truth in a Photograph?
Paula Becker to her sister, Herma Becker, 1906

Is there more truth
    in a photograph?

I ask myself –

I ask you Herma
    as the camera clicks
in your hands – as you take
pictures of me
        secretly at night –
I am nude – posing with fruits
and flowers – posing for myself,
        only for myself –

The light is harsh –
the shadows are grim –

But can truth be
        partly remembered?
Its texture felt beforehand
like an old dream, half-forgotten
        in our minds –
Or must it always surprise?

Yes, the light is harsh
and the shadows are grim –

And when the photographs arrive
        will I find truth?

When I examine the angles,
    the shapes between
this light and these fruits –
between my eyes and my mouth –
What will I find there?

Self-Portrait as a Life-Sized Nude
1906

At night
before the dance,
    the dancer stands
in a room full of shadows.

She surveys herself
    naked in the mirror,
her feet poised just so –

She holds herself straight, erect –
    her legs close together
her arms folded into
    the tension of her energy –
supple, pliant – her hands aligned
    between her breasts –

Fragrance of oranges –
    a fruit in each hand
to give shape to her fingers –
    A fruit in each hand
so she can find the balance
between the weight
    and the colour –

Before the dance:
her left foot slides forward –
    her right foot, behind,
perpendicular to the left –

Her thighs gather in
    all her strength
before the dance –
    The silk of her muscles
contained – suspended
    yet taut within her stillness –

Fragrance of oranges –
    her fingers curled around
ripe fruit –

68

Self-Portrait as a Standing Nude with a Hat
1906

A brush stroke
and my face disappears –
and so do my nipples.

What is this desire
to become featureless –
        to become a menhir?
Why this yearning
to return to rock, to stone – ?

A brush stroke
and I can decide my fate.

I am painting myself into a menhir,
into the truest stance –

From the light in the colours
        you can see
that I am still flesh – not stone
not even rose marble – and I am so far away
                        from pink granite –

My face is gone
but I wear a hat with long ribbons
            to show you
that I'm still alive.
The long ribbons streaming
down my back show you
that this body is not flat.

It will take time to become stone.

But for now
I need these colours:

Look at the lemon in my left hand
            right between my breasts –
Look at the orange in my right hand
         held further down
a bit below my waist –

My face is gone
but my pubic hair
         remains.

A brush stroke
and I can decide my fate –

Self-Portrait Wearing a Blue
and White Striped Dress
1906

The dress itself
makes one think of summers
        in France –
picnics in Brittany –

The blue and white fragrance
      of the Atlantic –

Right hand on my chin.
Not a fist.
Fingers outstretched –
lightly touching my chin –
      Lightly –
I am not tired.

Can't you see
how serious I am, Rodin?

Imagine if I said that
     to *him*.

Yes, he would say, too serious
for a woman.
No, I would answer, I have to be
more serious than a man.

The sun blazes on my dress
    making it more
dazzling – but I stand aside
silent – and I need
    to be alone.

Self-Portrait with Yellowish Green
1906

Parrot green, lime green,
      pistachio green,

    yellowish green – bright
on your chin where your hand rests,
the left hand again –
    And there across your eyelids
        more green –

Is it the light?
Or is it a shadow?

Your ears are dark pink: sunburnt, stubborn –

Colours of madness, people will say,
      colours of insanity –

But if you tell them what you really think
they will turn away, afraid –

Two Girls: One Sitting in a White Shirt.
The Other; A Standing Nude
1906

Beauty that is Italian –
        The older sister has it –
Twelve-years-old,
her gestures are always so strong:
the way she tosses her head,
shaking her thick black hair
        out of her face –
The way she laughs, lifting her chin
at such an angle and glancing
out of the corners of her eyes –
Her white shirt flashing –
while pink oleanders just outside
the window brush fragrance
                against the wind –
And now she is so excited, so
happy as she surveys
her younger sister, who is five
and stands naked beside her.
It is the nakedness of a child, of a girl
who has been sick for a long time
and has just emerged from bed –
Her face closed with illness,
her flaxen hair damp with sweat –
Now her older sister bends towards her
saying, today you have no fever –
        today, you are cured –
The older sister keeps
        breaking the silence
saying, come here, I will help you,
come here, I have already
prepared your bath – While pink oleanders
just outside the window
brush fragrance against the wind –

Two Girls: Nude, One Standing, the Other
Kneeling in Front of Red Poppies
1906

The poppies glow with poison –
Red breathing black – in full bloom –
dark opium falls across
    the innocence of lemons,
the innocence of little girls
    who wait for butterflies –

It is so hot, they have left
    their clothes in the house –
Sheltered by huge poppies
they play naked in the garden – they play
beside a fountain you cannot see –
One standing, the other kneeling,
they examine a lemon – probe
an orange – undecided
    about what to do –
Who will fetch the knife
from the kitchen? Who will
    cut the fruit?
Will the orange
be sweet enough? Won't the lemon
    be too sour, too bitter?
Who will fetch the knife?
The knife they are forbidden
to touch – Time is endless –
    they think such poppies
will shelter them forever –

Two Girls with their Arms Across their Shoulders
1906

Sometimes the dark girl
is shorter – she has a story
to tell, a secret that rises
like a cloud of smoke –

A secret that is silver grey
like the dots on her blue dress.

A secret that lives with olive trees.

The two sisters continue
walking with their arms
across their shoulders –

A scarlet ribbon in her black hair –
a purple ribbon in her blonde hair –

Forgetting the beauty of her white dress,
the tall blonde girl listens
        and listens –

Ribbons curled up into bows,
curled up like resting butterflies –
while the secret unravels
stretching out before them
so they have to follow it –

Surrounded by silver grey,
they trace a secret that never ends –

Self-Portrait on a Hot Day in Paris
1906

Your face is flushed
    from the heat –

Skin of a ripe peach.
Skin of a goldfish in the sun.

The cry of the peacock
    is in your eyes –
        peacock blue
peacock green behind you –
as if you stood
in front of those bright feathers.

But there is no reprieve.
No respite from the heat.
Your face fills up the canvas –
There's hardly any background
hardly any green
        to look at.

Your face is flushed
    with anger – your eyes
outlined with a godly blue:
    lapis lazuli glows
against your burning skin.

How far can you go?
How far before you get blisters,
before your skin comes off?

How far will you go
before you peel off this face
    and begin again?

You have no time for anyone.
No time to justify yourself.
You cannot wait. You do not care
whether it will rain tonight
or tomorrow. The heat will not
keep you from working.

And your anger must
have a chance to breathe.

Self-Portrait as a Mask
1906

Eyeless – and so it is a mask.

As if I have lifted off my face –
the lines and shadows and shape
of my face – and placed it
      on a newspaper
for you to look at.

You might say
I have discarded my face
for you to examine.

No eyes – just holes –
    so it is not all of me –

This is my shell –
my own mask, my daily mask
that I create over and over again –

Today, the mask has reached
      a certain perfection:
look at this firm jaw
      these perfect lips –
and the flesh on these cheekbones
of such classic proportions –
never changing, never moving –

Here is a forehead that dreams
      only of eternity –

But how can human eyes
      live with such a lack
        of emotion – ?
Perhaps my eyes have died.
Or have they
      simply disappeared?

Self-Portrait with a Hat and Veil
1906

In this hat and veil,
    in this sheer yellow veil,
I am Eurydice
  in hell –

Eurydice in a room
in a hell where the curtains are as red
as poppies in the sun –
as red as the ripe seeds
Persephone once bit into.

And she has taken charge now –
She has smuggled in
the scent of orange blossoms,
brought in bolts of sea-green light –
and the sea air
    with turquoise shadows –

Sometimes I feel as if
I am underwater.

I chose to come here.

But I am doomed.
Doomed to hold on
to these oddly coloured roses
in my hand – pinkish lavender –

Pinkish lavender jarring against
the red curtains, the red panels
of the hat around my ears –

Pinkish lavender: the last two roses
    Orpheus left behind
for me – If only he had
given me flowers that were white
or even yellow –
    then I wouldn't
feel so conspicuous,
so out of place –

Self-Portrait, Frontal, with a Flower
in the Right Hand
1906/07

This is my face that greets me
in a dream – out of focus – it is
a face seen through fog, mist –
a face seen through rain, through
a rain streaked windowpane – How smudged
it is and blurred as if by accident,
as if I could not find the lines
          of my own face.

This is the face that Otto must see
nowadays – out of focus – fading away –
for I have left him for good.
I stand before plum coloured flowers:
Huge bushes – these rhododendrons –
And in my right hand I hold
a tiny white flower for Otto.
'Let me go.' I wrote to him –
'Let me be free.' And he will take
the white flower with its whitish stem –
almost ashen the way I painted it.
He will call it his little white rose
not knowing that it is a weed
                    mimicking jasmine –
He will call it his small snowdrop of petals
not knowing the petals are wild –
And the whiteness will remind him of moonlight.

And even now as I
          return to him, uncertain –
I make a necessary compromise –
          And even now
he will look at me and say
'At last –
     at last you have come back.'

But he will never notice
that my face has changed,
          that my face has become
     unreachable –
forever out of focus
               for him –

A White Horse Grazing in Moonlight
Paula Becker to Otto Modersohn
a retrospective view of 1901

A white horse
        grazing in moonlight –

That was our love –

And instead of giving you
        a deep red rose
I signed my initials
        in blood red paint –

That was our love –

I wrote '1901'
        in bright red paint –

A colour wrung
from the hearts of roses –
        I'm sure –

And you watched me
as I undressed
        as I stood naked
in the field – letting moonlight
        cover my skin –

Don't remind me.

Don't ask me
        for such love again.

Otto with a Pipe
Paula Becker to Otto Modersohn, 1906/07

Otto with a pipe.

Otto with a straw hat
in profile, facing right.

Otto with spectacles, frontal.

Otto sleeping.

Otto reading at his desk –
one hand supporting his head.

Otto with a pipe, in profile.

My private litany.

I could never
            truly find you.
You never let me.

Why did I love you?

Self-Portrait with a Lemon
1906/07

In the shade, especially
in the shade, when she stood
like that against the light –
in the shade, her face
looked darker,
darker than it really was –
and her arms
exposed to the sun all morning
glistened with sweat.

The noise of insects
prickled across the air –
    the windless air –
the heat opening and opening
skin, cell by cell, all the way
            down, deeper –
silt, marrow –
where Death cries out
hoping the soul will listen –

From the terrace
she could be seen
walking between the rows
of lemon trees –
now pausing, now turning around,
looking for something – maybe
waiting for someone –

The parrots were hiding.
The crows were somewhere else.
A child screamed – sulking,
raging – a baby cried –
And it was the time of day
when the temple bells
            were silent.

But there was movement
            within the silence.
A movement in the waiting –
A movement in the watching –
More than a gesture –

The blue border
on the end of her sari
            covering her head
cast a blue shadow –
a soft, cotton blue shadow
            across her face –
And there, where the blue darkness
                of her sari
met the darkness of her hair –
was another shadow,
another border – it was
a fast brush stroke – thick cobalt
blue disappearing into a maroon, ochre black –
                an orange, olive black –
a hungry blue
    plunging into black –

A brush stroke so fast
            and so strong
there was only one chance
of getting it right –

When she bit into the lemon in her hand
and lifted her head like that,
the sari-end slipped off
            of her hair
and she left it
hanging down for a moment –
then pulled it taut
over her shoulders instead –

The green light from the leaves
flickering across her throat –
The cobalt blue living within the kohl
streaked around her eyes –

Afterwards
she threw the rind far away –
almost out of the orchard –
and then she held up
another lemon to the light,
the light she hid from
as she stood there
        beside the trees –

Self-Portrait with a Sprig of Camellia Leaves
1906/07

I am Egyptian now –
darker than the sun can ever
            make me –

Burnt umber, burnt sienna
                under a pale blue sky –

And I hold this sprig of glossy leaves –
                evergreen, glabrous –

I hold this sprig
        for Death –

Look, I will say, to Death
take these leaves
        and smell them –

    smell them –

And What Will Death Do?
1906/07

And what will Death do?

What did he do in Faiyum?

Did he welcome the portrait
of each new mummy, saying yes,
yes, I recognize you –
I have seen this necklace before.

Did he kiss each portrait,
fingering the linen, the wood –
　　　saying yes –
let the soul be free from the body.

Did he stare into their open eyes
saying, yes, I will let your spirit return
to your body – In my Kingdom
　　　I will let you
　　　　　keep these leaves –

Did he unfasten a door
open a window, saying, come
over here – saying, look at this – ?

Self-Portrait with Two Flowers in the Left Hand
Paula Becker to Clara Westhoff, 1907

Now that I am truly ripe
with child – I don't have the strength
to paint myself naked before a mirror.

If I could, I would go
        to Paris right now –

Clara, you write to me from Berlin,
        from Oberneuland –
but you speak of Rilke's letters,
 Rilke's words
        full of Cézanne's light –

Cézanne's big exhibition in Paris –
    where I should be with *you* –
will soon be over.
And I won't make it this time.

From my eyes, my swollen eyelids,
you can tell how heavy I must be,
        how lethargic –

So now I wait for you
to bring me Rilke's letters,
        the ones you promised –
I need Rilke's words
to bring Cézanne into my room
        in Worpswede –

As for me,
I give you colours of crockery.

I wear a sleepy blue:
    blue of a ceramic milk jug –

Even the sky looks milky today.

Two flowers because
                of the second heart
beating within me.

My left hand because it has to be.

I want this child.

These flowers are for you, Clara –
for you, Cézanne –

Who has just Died?
Clara Westhoff to Paula Becker, 1908

Mornings I wake up wondering
        who just died –
and then I remember
        it was you –

I wake up wanting to touch you
wanting to
        take you into my arms –

Today
I thought of that winter afternoon
almost three years ago –
that afternoon we spent
by the stove in your small atelier
at the Brünjes –
how you kept the fire going,
throwing in little pieces of turf,
the oven door squeaking
each time you opened it –
And how you wept,
telling me that you could not
live in Worpswede – how you longed
for 'the world', for Paris –
And I held you – I can still
feel your shoulders, your back
under my hands – your hair,
your wet face –

Nine months have passed.
Still, I wake up confused
        in the middle of the night
wondering who
    has just died –

These days I am reading
The Discourses of Gautama Buddha –
trying to understand *maya* –
        But I cannot

let go of you – We should be
reading this book together
discussing it the way we went over
Nietzsche's *Zarathustra* –

Today it rained all day
 and I turned towards
the bust I made of you
long ago in 1899, remember –
when we had just met –
Suddenly I felt that the shoulders
were all wrong – and I wanted
to rework your face
 to leave it the way I knew you,
the way I saw you last –
Perhaps you would laugh
but I wanted to give it
 the 'great simplicity'
that you reached for –
But then again, maybe I only wanted
 to touch your face again –

Through the Blackness
Clara Westhoff's bust of Mathilde (Tille) Modersohn, 1915
Clara Westhoff to Paula Becker

Paula, your daughter is seven –
        she's almost eight now.
She came to me this morning –
her clothes smelling of sadness.

Paula, if we had known
        each other as children
then perhaps this is how
        I would remember you.

When Tille walked up to me
I felt it was you
        stepping out
of a photograph
        from your childhood –

She has your face,
        your golden red hair –

She sat so still
as I walked around my atelier
watching her face, studying the way
she held herself, the way
        she sat in my chair –
while the clay grew warmer,
more pliant in my hands –

She answered my questions
so earnestly – I wanted to laugh –
And I wondered, what were you like
        as a child?

And then, as I continued
working, forming Tille's face,
        your face, I couldn't help thinking –
as I continued moulding Tille's mouth
her chin – I remembered the night

93

we had walked along the river,
along the Weser – It was late –
It was the first warm night in May
but so dark, a new moon
                darkness everywhere –
And suddenly from the other side
of the river a nightingale called out –
Its song so sharp
     we stopped talking.
It sang out again and again
each note ringing, resounding
            through the blackness –
You held my arm –
Remember how we stood there
listening – amazed that we could hear it
so clearly across the water –
And how we felt that nightingale
        was calling out to us –

21 November 1916
Munich, Clara Westhoff to Paula Becker

You died
a day before
my twenty-ninth birthday –
but the news of your death
     reached me late –
I was in Berlin.

And when I returned
     to Worpswede
on the last day of November
with dead leaves
     in my hands –
dark brown and yellow –
     and a branch
of red berries – for the colour –
when I returned to Worpswede
your house was empty.

Otto had left.
Your sister, Milly
had taken the baby.

I had asked my brother
to place a bowl filled with fruits
     at your grave –
pears, figs, pomegranates –
Southern fruits
you would have painted.

Later, your mother wrote
to me with such joy
about finding those fruits
as if those fragrant colours
were the trick to bring you back –
as if you would return
     any day, any minute –

What did I feel
as I walked down that straight
flat road, surrounded by birch trees –
your trees – ? What did I feel?
Rainer always asks.

I felt nothing.
I was numb – frozen.

That was nine years ago.
But how can I ever forget?
How can I celebrate
        my life today
without lighting a candle
        for you?

Rainer came by this evening
to be with me again
after so many years –
Because of you he needs
to speak with me.
Whenever he wants
        to talk about you
he comes to me.

Tonight he brought your journals,
all your unpublished letters
sent to him by your mother.
He wanted my help,
my advice – should he edit
        your writing?
Start reading, he said.
That was my birthday present.

I made a pot of tea
        and then another –
We sat up late into the night
reading your words – Hardly talking –

Later
    Rainer kept saying, where is Paula?
But *where* is Paula?
This is not really her.
The person in these letters
is too sweet, he complained –
Paula was sharper, harder
in reality – There must be
    something missing.
I disagreed. Although
he was partly right.

I remembered our first time
    together in Paris –
Why didn't you write
about our visit to Vollard's gallery?
About Cézanne's paintings
on the floor, leaning against
the wall – How you looked through
them over and over again,
quickly and then slowly –
You held up
so many paintings for me
there in the dark corner –
Canvas after canvas of French colours
we had never even lived.

Why didn't you write
about that? Should it remain
    a secret?

Rainer wants me
to tell him your stories,
    our stories
that you never spoke of.

And I imagined him
writing your life
    in his words –

I remembered your old anger
at him for putting his words
    into my mouth –

And so, this time
I remained silent –
I refused to explain anything.

Of course, we fought again
over you. I defended you.

Tonight, I decided
that I will make sure
my journals are not seen
    by anyone
for a long time
    after my death.

The Room Itself is Dying
Clara Westhoff to Rainer Maria Rilke, circa 1921

Upstairs the glass glitters
today – windowpanes hysterical
with sun – I know there is
sunlight pouring in
through the gable windows – sunlight
warming the wooden floor –

But I cannot bear to look.

Once we planned this house together –
Remember – after the war –
You blessed this house
with a poem – a little charm you composed
         to keep us safe, to keep us
together – A little charm
      that does not work.

And now
this extra room on top,
      the 'gable room'
that I had saved for you –
for you to live in, write in –
      for you to be sheltered
in your solitude – this room
you have never seen –
      It is dying.

The room itself is dying
of emptiness –

It is April now –
spring even in Fischerhude.
The wind hisses, suddenly restless
through trees, flinging branches
ripping half-opened leaves –
The river quickens – Our daughter
has forgotten your face –
She says you have none.

Another year has gone by
    and still you do not
come to see us.

There are days
when I think if Paula were still
alive and if she lived here
in this village, or nearby
in Worpswede – if Paula
    were still alive –
then, surely you would
        arrive at the station
loaded down with your books
and papers – Then, no doubt
you would come to see Paula –
And perhaps that way, I imagine,
        in her presence
you would allow me
to speak with you –

But she is dead –
she who had brought us together
        so many times
without even knowing that she did –

Ruth's Wish

Clara Westhoff's posthumous bust of Rilke, 1936
Clara Westhoff to Rainer Maria Rilke

It was our daughter's wish –
      Ruth wanted me
to make a new bust of you –
of you when you were older.
She wanted something more
      than a photograph
to remember you by –

How far can memory go,
      how deep –
          and still be fair?
Can there be truth
      without love?

This time
I lift your head up –
I raise it – Monumental –
Your eyes half-closed,
you are lost within yourself –
Your face is fuller,
      your hair thinning –
You are beardless.
Your lips are pressed together.
There is something implacable –
      a sternness I knew.

You look firm.
    But I know
you are still dreaming –

16 April 1945
Clara Westhoff to Paula Becker

Three years ago
when the first bombs
        started to fall
on Bremen – I tried to move
closer to God.

But it's you I talk to most
        in my mind.

I am stuck in Fischerhude.

Today, the merchant Oelze
stopped by with a bundle of papers.
Manuscripts – he said,
poems by a man called Gottfried
Benn – I must keep
            everything safe.

So I opened my iron chest
        again.

And now Oelze's papers lie
with Rainer's Cézanne letters,
Rainer's sonnets and elegies –

Bremen is no more.
Oelze told me –

But tonight I will sit with you,
with my memories –

All those letters
    about Cézanne,
Rainer sent me
were really written for you.
    I always knew.
And in the end he meant
the sonnets to be for you –

And the elegies, he wanted to place
in a niche to your memory, he said –

Always you.

He loved Lou
and he loved you, Paula –
He needed you.

It was your death he kept
within his heart – your death
he could never accept.

Was it the Blue Irises?
Kunsthalle Bremen, 1985

The way I returned again and again to your self-portrait with blue
    irises
made the guards uneasy.

The way I turned away from your self-portrait with blue irises
made the guards uneasy.

Was it the blue irises floating around your face, was it
your brown eyes illuminated by something in the blue irises?

How could you know, how could you feel all this
that I know and feel about blue iris?

I was on the top floor with other paintings, other painters,
but unable to concentrate on them because
already I could hear the tone of voice your brown eyes would
    require.

So I rushed back down to be with you.

The look that passed between us must have lasted
a long time because I could smell the light
from the irises falling across your face.

The look that passed between us was full
of understanding so I could imagine living with you
and arguing with you about whether to put garlic in the soup.

I stared at the blue irises but in my throat
there was the pungent fresh bitterness of watercress.

When I finally left you I noticed three guards following me.

By the time I got home I was furious at them
for witnessing all this.

Clara's Voice

Written after listening to a 1953 recording
of Clara Westhoff reading Rilke's early poems.

Old woman
reading a young man's poems –
your Northern accent
        softened
with Low German consonants –

How often have I listened
to your voice
trying to understand you.

Trying to imagine
        the young woman
you were – Six feet tall –
        reserved but impulsive –

A woman who once danced
        for hours with sailors
on the deck of a stranded ship
until you had to be carried off
        with blisters on your feet –

Later, they called you 'die Rilke' –
celebrating you for having been
his wife – Inviting you
to read his poems, to speak
    of the man you knew.

And you obliged
the public – afraid to disappoint,
reluctant to say
        what you really thought.

In this recording you sound
like a grandmother –

Listening to your gentle
intonation, your patience –
        I imagine you
reading stories to your grandson.

Lines Written in Venice
about a visit to Mathilde (Tille) Modersohn
Bremen, 1995

Where else but in Venice
should this memory
be written down.

It was my first visit –
I brought you summer flowers –
Pale pink roses, dark irises –
Not knowing that all afternoon
you would sit in a corner
              by the window –
not knowing that beside you
on the wall there would be
a painting by your mother
with those roses – precisely –
as if the painting were a mirror
reflecting the newly arranged
          flowers on the table –

Looking at your face
I imagined if Paula had lived
to be old – then this is how
she would have looked,
          like you –
Your hair faded but still long
worn pulled back
      and coiled exactly
the way Paula used to
          style her hair.

Your walls were covered
with Paula's paintings – your rooms
filled with Paula's things –
porcelain vases, a decorated box –
      and the chandelier
with a baroque angel,
an angel surrounded by a wreath
of candles, a garland

of tall slender candles –
The chandelier Paula had lit
minutes before she died.

Here in Venice
there's the sound of water
slapping against boats –
some docked, others
far into their journeys –
November sun burns
             across old glass
window panes – sparkling,
piercing – Colours stunned
and rippling with reflections
as if the glass were melting –
Dark yellow paint, ochre
and burnt reddish brown
crumbles off houses –
Houses seem to lean over
the water – small bridges
connect narrow streets –
Mazes, cracked stones –
Stones, wet and chilled
    from the water –

It's your birthday
today – I've spent the morning
walking, getting lost –
remembering you,
how you liked to travel.

Once in a bank in New York
the man standing behind you
happened to notice your name
written on your passport –
'Modersohn'.

Modersohn? He said, asking you
about Paula. When he realised
she was your mother, he told you
about his escape from the Nazis
with one of her paintings –

But when he arrived in New York
   he had to sell it
      to survive –

He told you he felt honoured
to meet you – invited you
to his home in Brooklyn –
But you felt so guilty
   so responsible
for German history
that you could not
   bear to visit him.

And then I remembered your openness –
The story about two women,
   complete strangers
who had knocked on your door –
   you welcomed them –
And after they left
you noticed they had torn out
pages from your mother's
   cookbook – pages
in which she had written
her intimate thoughts –

All your stories
are so entangled in my mind –

And now, necklaces of Venetian glass
remind me of your cousin's daughter,
my friend, who is more like a niece to you –
   I think of her,
the bright colours she likes to wear.

I remember her gift to me
after your death:
The photograph of you
newborn and asleep
while Paula holds you –
   while Paula looks up
at the camera –
The photograph

that you kept in your room –
the photograph in your old
white frame, the frame slightly battered
        and not so white anymore –
I've kept that photograph
        in your frame –
it hangs in my room now
right above my desk –

Fischerhude, 2001
Café im Rilke-Haus

Clara, your house
      is a café now –
Restored, preserved –
and named for one
      who never entered it –

Thick green, the grass in September –

Horses step out of the fog –

A stream from the Wümme
      still flows by your garden –

I drink tea and stare
      out the window –

And I have a stone in my pocket –
      a stone and an acorn –

Worpswede, 2001
for Hille Darjes

Und wer ist das Mädchen?
Das war meine Mutter.

Full moon
        in September –
Three weeks too early
to be a true harvest moon –

But look,
        still low in the sky
that moon behind thick clusters
            of birch trees –
pale yellow
    as if it were a huge melon
ripening on a vine, entangled
                in the grass –

All afternoon
    I walked past fields
between museums, past so many trees,
birches, oaks – remembering you, Paula –
your paintings, your colours
                burnt in my mind –
Today I thought of you
    with so much pain –
as if it were 1907, 1908 –
            and you had just died –
as if you had been
my dear friend, my sister –

Later, I listened
        to your grandniece
reading from your journal,
your letters – She wore your brooch –
She has your power.

Later, we sat together
looking through her old album –

photographs of you,
of your entire family –

Who is this?
And who is this? I kept
        asking –

That was Paula's brother
        in Indonesia.
That was the woman
who loved him so much –

And who is that girl?
That was my mother –